Here we met
the baby whale

Sheep

Sheep

Seagull Point

Einar Runde's forest

Uncle Jakob's
boat→

Uncle Jakob's
house

Cormorant Rock

Telephone
←and Telegraph

Uncle Johan's
house

Postoffice

Boat houses

Jarle's house

Store

Community hall

School

Fish storehouses

The harbor

Breakwater
(the nets lie here for drying
and repair)

Lobster bank

The Royal Post Boat

Uncle Johan's
salmon grounds

Sonia AND Tim Gidal

BY THE SAME AUTHORS:

My Village in Austria

My Village in India

My Village in Yugoslavia

My Village in Ireland

PANTHEON

MY VILLAGE
IN NORWAY

Franklin I.M.C.

My name is Jarle Hjoerungdal, and I live in Norway, on the island of Runde. There are one hundred and fifty thousand islands along our coast, and my home is on one of them. Runde Island means round island. When you see it from a ship out in the Atlantic Ocean it looks round, and so it was given that name by my forefathers at the time of the Vikings.

I can see the ocean from every point on the island. The ocean is really what we live by. In Norway, the soil never gives enough food for the people, because our country consists mainly of mountains and forests and glaciers. There is a good farming section in eastern Norway, but otherwise there is no fertile soil except along the *fjords*. That's why so many Norwegians become fishermen or sailors, or merchant mariners. Sailing the seven seas in oil tankers and whalers and freighters, they go to many foreign lands. We have the third-largest shipping fleet in the world, right after America and England.

My Viking forefathers were boatbuilders and traders. But often they went to distant countries as invaders and conquerors, and came back from their expeditions with a lot of loot.

Two hundred people live on our island. And there are more than three hundred sheep, as well as fifty cows and thirty horses—and a great many birds.

On a high cliff near our lighthouse, over a million sea gulls nest in spring and summer, and about thirty thousand puffins lay their eggs on the mountains. On the rocks in the sea live six hundred big cormorants and many auks, and the oyster catchers are all over the beaches, except if you come close. You never catch *them!*

Forty-six different kinds of birds nest on our islands, among them many rare ones.

In winter, when I look out of my window, I see the herring fleet on the sea. Hundreds of fishing boats are out then, and the sky is dark with sea gulls hunting for herring too.

The Gulf Stream goes by our coasts. It keeps our waters free from ice, and the herring come close to the coast in the warm current.

Often I see big ocean liners passing by, and the seal hunters coming back from the North Polar regions.

2

Uncle Jakob is the skipper on one of them, and he always puts in at Runde harbor after a hunting expedition.

Father isn't a fisherman. He repairs lighthouses along the coast. He is away from home half of the year. So, for six months every year, Mother and my sisters Aase and Eli, and little Trygve and I are alone, and I help with all the work around the house.

Today, I am on my way home from a trip to the *fjords* and *fjells* of Sunmoere County. My teacher, Per Mikklebust, had gone there with my friends and me, and we spent the night on the Royal Mailboat in the harbor of Aalesund city.

I woke up with a start. The ship's horn was blowing so loud, I nearly rolled off the bench I was sleeping on.

I hear my friend Paul cry out in his sleep: "Ho! Let's go! Ho! Let's go!"

I shake him awake, and he sits up on the bench and rubs his eyes.

"Where shall we go, Flinky?" I ask. Flinky is Paul's nickname, because he is really smart and quick. "Flink" means just that in our language.

"I must have been dreaming," Flinky says. "I was having a fight with two gauchos in the pampas—it *must* have been in South America —and then one of them hit me with a dried fish over my helmet. It made an awful noise in my head."

"You smelled fish, and you heard the ship's horn, Paul, that's all, and you probably banged your head on the bench."

The horn gives the second blast, and the ship's engines start pounding. The engine room is right underneath our benches, and the benches rattle, but my cousin Jan and our teacher Per Mikklebust are still sleeping. We have been four days in the *fjord* country, climbing over the hairpin bends up to the Stairways of the Trolls, and to the whaling station near Mikklebust village, where Teacher Mikklebust comes from. The Royal Mailboat is named *Sigurd*.

I know the captain well, because the *Sigurd* comes to Runde every day. It is the only connection between our island and the mainland. Captain Andersen let us board the ship last night while it was in harbor at Aalesund for repairs, so we didn't have to go to a hotel.

I didn't sleep much. All night long I heard the sea gulls screeching their shrill "kitty-veek, kitty-veek!" I heard thousands of them, fighting for a place on the window sills of the fish storehouses around the quay. And does that harbor smell! It smells of fresh fish and of rotting fish, and of oil and of sea gull droppings. But now we move, and the breeze comes through the porthole, and chases the smell out.

We are soon on the open sea. Teacher Per and Jan have waked up at last. Teacher Per turns up his nose and says, "There's an awful smell in the cabin, and it must come from my whale-fin spine. I should get hot water and soap and wash it again, or else throw it out through the porthole. But I certainly won't give it up." He had got it yesterday at the whaling station we visited. We waited six hours, and then a whaling boat came in at last. A giant whale was towed alongside, with a chain around its tail.

The tail fin was eight feet across, and the whale weighed well over four thousand pounds, they told us. I had never seen a big whale before. Sometimes baby whales roam in the sea near us. We see them when we go out fishing in our small boats. They are harmless. But this big one did not look harmless at all, and I would not like to meet such a one when I am out in the fishing boat.

It took six men to cut up the whale. The meat was sent off at once in a cutter to the islands, for sale. Fresh whale meat tastes like beef, and not at all like fish. We had it for dinner three times during the last few weeks. But the blubber and the liver are much more important. From the blubber comes whale oil, and from whale oil they make margarine and soap. The people at the whaling station told us that our country produces more whale oil than any other country in the world.

There are only two whaling stations left in Norway, because the whale became scarce in the Arctic Ocean. Our whaling ships now go on long expeditions down to the seas in the Antarctic regions, and they have their factories right on board: the whale meat is canned there, and the oil is boiled, and from the whale liver they extract the vitamins to go into vitamin pills. The whales are spotted by air from helicopters the ships take along, and then they are caught with harpoon guns.

The tail fin of the whale I saw had hundreds of spines, each more than three feet long. I took one to hang on my wall. It really does smell a bit of rotting whale meat, but not as bad as my friends say.

We go up on deck. Captain Andersen sees us from the bridge, and invites us to go to the galley. There we get hot coffee and flatbread and brown cheese and pickled herring.

The mainland is drifting away, but the Aalesund sea gulls follow us. They sail through the air and dive quickly whenever leftovers from the galley are thrown overboard.

We beg some flatbread from the cook, and roll it with a bit of spit in our hands. I throw mine high into the air. The gulls swoop down with shrieking cries, and one of them catches it just before it drops into the sea. Now we throw pieces straight down to the water. But the sea gulls have sharp eyes, and they can maneuver much more quickly than we think. They stop in midair and drop like a bolt.

One big sea gull swoops close by my outstretched hand and tries to snatch a big piece of bread from me. I put the bread on a chest, and stand close to it.

"She can't take the bread from there in full flight," says Jan. "No use putting it on that chest; sea gulls are cheeky only in the air, they never dare stop near a human being."

"Let's wait and see," says Teacher Per. "Sea gulls are greedy, and they are afraid another one may snatch up what they don't catch. If we are patient, I think she will come and try to get that piece of bread."

The gull circles around us with angry screeches. We don't move. Again and again the bird tries to approach the bread in full flight, but she can't—there isn't enough space between the railing and us for her to fly through.

Twice she gives up with disgusted squeals, but she always comes back again. The big piece of bread tempts her—and then, suddenly, the sea gull stands on the chest, her wings spread wide as in flight, and now she has the bread in her beak. It is much too big for her to

swallow at once. The bird looks at us angrily. She flaps her wings, gets herself airborne, and makes off right past our faces, so that we draw back with a start.

"That was quite a feat!" says Teacher Per. He takes out his notebook, and writes in it. Per is a zoologist. He studies the habits of birds and their different calls and customs, where they come from in spring, and where they migrate to in fall.

A wall of fog appears on the sea, and we head right into it. The *Sigurd* starts rolling.

"Let's go on the bridge and visit the captain," I say to Paul.

"It's bumpy enough where I am right now," he answers. "It will be worse up there," and he stretches out on a piece of canvas and moans. Paul always moans when the sea gets rough. He thinks the seasickness will pass him by then. But I climb up to the bridge; I never get seasick.

Captain Andersen is turning the wheel and looking at the compass and chart in front of him.

"How about it, Jarle, my boy—do you think you could steer her in this fog?" he asks me.

"I would like to try, sir," I answer. I take the wheel and bring the compass needle in line with my direction on the chart. I look through the window, but there is only fog; I don't see a thing.

The captain gives his commands through the speaking tube to the engine room.

"Slow down now!" he calls into the tube, and presses the foghorn button three times. "Keep her straight!" is the command to me. But that isn't so easy, with the engines being cut, and I am quite glad when Captain Andersen says, "Thank you, my boy, you did a neat job," and takes over again.

After a while, the sea calms down, and the fog lifts as quickly as it came. Out of the mist appears our island, Runde. It really *does* look round from the distance.

"Do you see the Handmarks?" asks Captain Andersen. "They stand out very clearly now!" I see the deep impressions in the left and right ends of the mountains of Runde very well from where I stand.

"Do you know where that name comes from?" Captain Andersen asks. We don't, but they really do look as if a giant had squashed the island rocks between his fists and left his handmarks there.

"There's an old legend about it," Captain Andersen says. "Runde Island, so it says, wasn't always there. You know that our country became Christian under the Viking king, St. Olav. Now, one day he came sailing out of Aalesund, the way we are going today. Over there, on the Ulstein Mountains, lived a powerful Ulstein troll. St. Olav tried to make him into a Christian, but the troll jeered at him and chased him off his territory.

"St. Olav sailed on, and as he went he called back to the troll on his mountain: 'There will be Christians here one day, just where I am sailing now!'

" 'Dead ones!' shouted the troll, and he got so furious that he tore the mountain under him out of the sea and flung it through the air into the ocean, at St. Olav.

"The mountain hit the sea far away from St. Olav's ship and sank down with a mighty splash. Only the top is still visible—it is your island, Runde! And the Handmarks on the sides of your island are the impressions from the hands of the giant troll."

The captain steers the *Sigurd* through the small harbor entrance and alongside the landing pier. We say *"God dag"* and climb down from the bridge to the foredeck. Jan and Teacher Per are standing there, waving to our friends on land.

I see my horse Thor grazing, and there is Father working in our little field in front of the house, and my sister Aase waves a handkerchief out of the kitchen window.

Our house stands on a slope near the post office, less than a hundred yards from the shore.

Nothing grows behind our house or on the slopes, except wild moss which the sheep eat, and wild plants and berries. Grass grows only on the narrow strip between the mountain and the sea. The strip is fifty yards wide in some places, even two hundred yards in others, but never more than that.

Everybody in the village has his pasture land, for green fodder and for making hay for the horses and cows. All the milk we can spare is collected in the morning by the island's one truck and is sent on the *Sigurd* to Aalesund—more than a hundred quarts every day. The truck travels on the only road we have on the island. The road passes most of the houses, and is about five miles long.

My classmates Oddvar and Bjoern and Randulf are standing on the road, near the new schoolhouse. My cousin Hans-Jakob is with them, and I wave to them.

Uncle Johan and his cousin Birger are waiting on the jetty, with wooden crates packed tightly with salmon. Every morning the salmon caught around Runde is sent off to Aalesund city. Aalesund is really the biggest fishing center of all Norway, and from there the fish is sold to places all over the world.

I take my rucksack and my whale fin, and we go down over the gangplank. The crew of two unloads wooden poles for making haystacks, and empty milk cans, and the mail of course. Slate tiles for the roof of our new school have come, too, and two bicycles and a few boxes with salt and sugar and fruit cans, for Ingvald Runde's Landhandel (country store). It is the only store on the island.

When we reach the end of the landing pier, the *Sigurd*'s whistle blows, and she is already heading for the open sea again, back to Aalesund.

On the road, our friends are waiting to tell us the news:

"There was a big storm in the south!" Hans-Jakob says. "They phoned from Oslo last night, Jarle. Your father is leaving soon. They need him, because there was a lot of damage to the lighthouses, and all repairmen have been called south."

That's bad. I thought I would work with Father next week, re-building my room and making it bigger. Now it will have to wait till next summer.

Paul comes along. On the way we meet the horses Fritjof and Lekanoey. Lekanoey belongs to Einar Runde, the man who set out our island forest, and Fritjof belongs to Uncle Johan. I think it is the most beautiful horse on our island. When Uncle Johan's great-grand-father bought his first horse, he named it Fritjof, and ever since, every horse in his family has been given the same name.

Our horses are small, with short legs. But they are strong and sturdy and very patient, and they have very fine manes, like the horses on the temples in ancient Greece in my school book. I like their cream color. The tips of their ears and their manes and tails have black markings, and they all have black legs.

I walk up to my house, and Paul goes home too.

"I'll be back soon, Jarle," he says as we part. "Ask your uncle if we can go salmon fishing with him this evening."

Father built our house all by himself, with only Grandfather and Uncle Johan to help him. My room is right under the roof. It is as small as a cabin on a herring schooner.

Right outside my window I put a birdhouse that I had built. For three years now, a black female starling has come back to it every spring. She eats worms and berries right out of my hand, and every year she has young ones. I watch them grow and learn to fly, and then in fall I see them join the big bird migration on the way south. But the mother comes back to my birdhouse again every spring.

"Jarle! Jarle!" my little brother Trygve calls from the kitchen.

"You've come at the right time," says my sister Aase. "*Frokost ferdig*—breakfast is ready!"

I put my rucksack and the whale fin down on the floor. In the kitchen, we sit around the big table, and Mama serves coffee and sandwiches with smoked salmon and hard-boiled eggs and *stikkelsbaer* jam made from the berries behind the house.

Teacher Per has come to say goodbye to Father. He is on his way to the puffin rocks, and has his camera with him. Mama asks him to take a family picture of us. We never had one with all of us together, and this is our last chance before Papa comes back from his trip.

Teacher Per lines us up, with our house in the background.

"Wait a minute!" Mother cries. "Let's put on our best pullovers for the family picture."

"Oh, why all this fuss?" says Father, but he too goes to put on the pullover Mother knitted for him. She and Aase knit all our pullovers, and they design them too; there are no two of them alike.

We line up again. But then Teacher Per asks us to shift position, because the sun is shining into his camera. Now we have the sea as a background, and Per says:

"You have so many colors in your pullovers, I will call the picture *Birds of Many Colors*."

We have to laugh, of course, and Per says:

"Thank you, I've snapped the picture!"

Teacher Per takes very good pictures, mostly of birds, when he is watching them out on the *fjells* and on the beaches.

"Jarle, I'm going out again tomorrow," he says. "I'm looking for young birds to put rings on their feet. You could come along and help me."

"Sure thing!" I answer. "When do we meet?"

"One o'clock, at Long Point," he tells me. He shakes hands with Father and wishes him a safe trip, and off he goes on his bicycle.

Our horse Thor grazes in the field. I put a rope around his head as a halter, jump on his back, swing one leg over, and that does it.

During the night Thor was born there was a great thunderstorm. That is why he was named Thor, after the ancient Norse god of thunder.

But our horse Thor is gentle and patient, like all our *fjord* horses. He lets me mount him without kicking or throwing me off, and I can ride him without a saddle—the way I like it best.

16

I ride over to the breakwater at the harbor. Uncle Johan is sitting on the stone mole, mending fishing nets.

"*God dag,* Uncle Johan!" I call to him. "Have you seen Hans-Jakob?"

"He is up in the drying room with Birger."

"Uncle, may I go in the boat with you today, and take Paul along?"

"Sure! Sure! I can use two strong Vikings this evening—we're taking the nets in!"

I often stay with Uncle Johan. His son is my best friend, and I like going to his house when Father is away. On Sundays we make music together. Uncle Johan plays the violin. His mother plays the harmonium they have in their house; I play my guitar, and the others sing to our music.

"I'll be back with Paul at five o'clock, Uncle," I say.

I turn Thor around, and ride over to the storehouses.

"Hoy!" I shout to my horse, and pull at the halter. "Stop!"—and I turn off the road quickly. I have seen Grandfather Ben from afar, and I'm sure he is feeding his pigs. That's just about all I need to bring Uncle Johan bad luck with the fish. Looking at a pig before going out to sea means you won't catch anything that day; you might as well stay home. Grandfather Ben always kept pigs. But he never caught a good salmon in all his life, people say. He gave up fishing long ago.

I make a detour, keeping behind the houses, and ride along the beach to the storehouses. Leaving Thor to graze, I climb up the dark wooden steps to the upper story.

Birger doesn't hear me coming, because the wind machine in the drying room is very noisy. He is standing near the glass door and admiring a big dried fish in his hands.

I tiptoe up to him and shout from behind into his ear:

"Oh, what a beauty of a codfish!"

Birger turns around. "Codfish yourself!" he calls out, and with the dried fish he slaps me where it hurts most, on the south side of my behind.

"Ouch!" I cry. "That hurts."

"That will teach you not to startle me," he says, laughing. "I wasn't admiring the beauty of the dried fish—I measured its length, and now I've tested it for hardness on your behind. Did it hurt much?"

"It certainly did! And it still smarts," I grumble.

"Fine!" says Birger. "That means the fish is hard enough for export to Cuba," and he throws it on a high pile. "A gaucho will enjoy it at some campfire in the pampas of South America. Let's see if the next one goes to Spain for a change."

"You are talking in riddles again, Birger," says Hans-Jakob. He comes out of the drying room pushing a rack of salted fish in front of him. And I ask why a fish that hurts me should go to Cuba instead of to Spain.

"I'll tell you," answers Birger, "if you can keep your ears open long enough to learn something new." Birger is really very fresh, and if he were not so tall I would tell him so to his face.

"You know these are all codfish. Uncle Johan brought them back from the Lofoten islands this spring; it was a big haul for everybody this year. We cut them open and clean them and salt them, and then they are stacked on the racks and stay for a while in the drying room, where hot air is blown around by the electric fans.

"After a few hours in there, Hans-Jakob helps me push the racks out and we put a new layer of salt on. I let the salt settle down for a few days, and then the fish go back into the drying room, and out again and in again and out again for weeks, till we get dizzy from pushing the racks in and out. In the end the fish are ready for export.

"Now, the Spaniards like their codfish at least sixteen inches long, and not too salty. The saltier the fish, the harder. But the Cubans want it very salty, and don't mind how long the fish is. The one I whacked you with was just under sixteen inches, so I wasn't quite sure where to put it. But it was already too hard for Spain, as you felt, and so I threw it on the pile for Cuba. Shall I test another one?"

"No, thank you very much!" I say. "I'm already an expert on that test. And anyway, I came for Hans-Jakob, to go lobster fishing with him. Let's get going."

We climb down the dark stairs and go home for *middag*.

Paul is working in the field, cutting grass.

"Flinky, it's time for *middag*," I call to him.

"*Ikke middag!*" he calls back. "No lunch for me till I have cut the

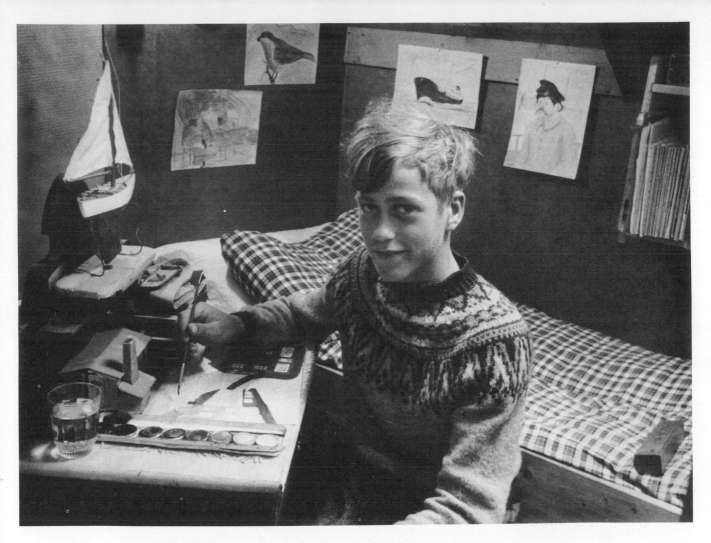

grass here. Father is hanging it up to dry back there. The sun is out—we want the grass cut and off the ground before the next rain spoils it. There's a south wind, it will dry fast today.

"I am going salmon fishing with Uncle Johan, Flinky. Will you come along?"

"Sure I'll come, what do you think? Five o'clock at the jetty?"

"Five o'clock—and don't look at a pig today," I say.

We have our main meal in the afternoon, at four o'clock. For lunch today, there is dried flounder, and bread and brown cheese, and sliced tomatoes and milk.

After *middag*, I go up to my room under the roof, and bolt the door. When I paint, I like to be alone. The table and chair are really too small for me. But if they were my size, the room would be too small for *them*.

21

I have pinned my paintings all over the walls: the *Sigurd* and that old sailor with the big mustache are my favorites. My starling I painted too, of course, sitting on a branch and singing. Now I start painting the harbor of Aalesund, with the fishing boats in, and the sea gulls sitting on the window sills, and the oily water shining purple and yellow and red.

I bought four new colors with the money I saved sleeping on the bench in the *Sigurd*. I paint in peace for a long time, but then Trygve knocks at the door and I let him in.

"May I borrow your sailing boat, Jarle?" he asks. He means the model I built.

"How do you know you won't lose it, the way you lost your *Kon Tiki?*" I ask. I had made a little model raft for Trygve that looked just like the raft on which Thor Heyerdahl and his friends went almost four thousand miles over the Pacific Ocean, all the way from South America to the South Sea Islands. Trygve had played with his model *Kon Tiki* on the beach, and had lost it.

"It wasn't my fault," says Trygve. "The big wave came so quickly, it went right over my head, and then the *Kon Tiki* was gone." He has tears in his eyes, and I console him.

"You know, Trygve, perhaps your *Kon Tiki* is on her way to the South Sea Islands right now. I am sure birds can rest on her, she's big enough for that, and one day somebody will find her on a beach far away, and read the words TRYGVE, RUNDE, NORWAY, and then he may send it back to you." I had cut these words into the little raft.

"Here, take my boat," I say. "But be sure never to let go of the long string, when you sail her on the beach. Fasten it to your belt."

Trygve promises and makes off, very happy indeed. But will he catch it if he loses my model ship!

"Mother, I am meeting Hans-Jakob. We're going to check the lobster pots. Have you got a polefish for me, for bait?"

"Take one from the bucket in the cellar," Mother says, "and bring me six lobsters for dinner. It's Father's last meal with us before he leaves. Tell Uncle Johan I'll pay for them when I see him."

"We'll be lucky if we catch as many as that. There are only ten pots out today."

"I am sure you will catch more. We are having a very good lobster season. Your Uncle Johan and Uncle Jakob have caught over two hundred in the last four days."

I put some string in my pockets and hang my polefish on a wire over the handlebars of my bicycle. Then I ride off, past the harbor and around the big bend to the cliffs. Hans-Jakob is in his boat, and we row out to the lobster rocks, where Uncle Johan has his grounds this year. Every fisherman has fishing rights on his own, special place, and that's the only place where he is allowed to put out his traps.

I take the oars and row until Hans-Jakob has brought up the first five pots, then we switch and he rows.

"Empty," he says, and lets the first pot slide back into the sea. A big stone in the wooden, barrel-shaped trap makes it sink down. But a glass buoy is attached to it with a long rope, to show where the trap lies on the floor of the sea, and we use the rope to haul the barrel up.

The lobsters live in the water among the rocks. They feed on oysters and snails. But fish is a delicacy for them. We put pieces of polefish into the pots as bait. The lobster crawls in and eats the fish, but it can't crawl out again—it is caught.

There is a big lobster in the second pot. Hans-Jakob grasps it by the back and holds it up. I take two pieces of string and tie the pincers tightly together. Now they can't nip any more, and we take the tiny roe off the underside of the lobster and eat it. Then we put the lobster in a box.

Hans-Jakob finds four lobsters, and I find three. That's a nice catch we have, from only ten pots.

We take our catch to Ingvald Runde. He weighs it—but then I remember Mother wanted six, and so I take six from the scales again. Ingvald Runde throws the seventh into the big salt-water tank in his storehouse. There are already hundreds and hundreds of lobsters in it. Landhandler Runde, as we call Ingvald, buys all the lobsters he can get. There are already more than one thousand lobsters in his tank, the catch from the last four days. A few hours before the boat to Aalesund comes in from the other islands, he packs them into big crates for shipment. But that he does only when he has heard from Aalesund by telephone that a foreign ship with lobster tanks is on her way into the harbor, to take the catch from all the islands to other countries.

This way, the lobsters are only a few hours without water. They are packed tightly into the crates, eighty-eight pounds to each crate, and the pincers are tied together, so they won't start fighting among themselves.

We ride home on our bicycles. I balance a box with the six lobsters on my handlebars.

"They will fall off!" says Hans-Jakob, but I laugh at him. Near my house, Hans-Jakob shouts suddenly:

"Look out! A wild pig!" I swerve sharply, and of course the box falls off. There is no pig, of course, and Hans-Jakob laughs like mad about his stupid joke. But my lobsters crawl all over the ground.

"You are just a *torsk*, a stupid codfish, fit to be salted!" I tell him, and he calls back, "And you are a big fat *sei*, a stupid coalfish!"

"*Torsken og seien gaar samme veien!*" somebody calls to us. "Codfish and coalfish go the same way." It is Uncle Jakob passing us on his way home, and he laughs. This is an old saying, because both fish are stupid and are easily caught, and mostly they are caught together.

Hans-Jakob pedals on with Uncle Jakob. They go the same way. I am mad at Hans-Jakob, that *torsk*. A *torsk* he is, *and* a *sei*. I pick my lobsters up and carry them up to the house. It is four o'clock, and time for Father's farewell dinner.

The six lobsters are the first course, and soon they are gone. Then we have *lapskaus*, a stew of meat and potatoes and onions. After that Mother brings the hot *hardinglefse*, or pancakes, from the electric stove, and we eat them with butter and jam and drink our coffee.

After the meal, we all reach out with our right hands, and touch each other over the center of the table. This is our way of saying thanks for the meal, and to wish each other good health.

Uncle Johan and his cousin Birger are already in their motorboat, and Cousin Paul and I climb in.

"Tokka-tokka-tokka . . . ," the motor starts up, and we speed out to Uncle Johan's fishing grounds. There are fourteen good salmon grounds in the waters around Runde Island, and as with the lobsters, the fishermen must keep to their own fishing grounds. Nobody else is allowed to use them.

The sea is rough today, and the boat is being tossed about like a nutshell. Paul and I sit in the stern, we bump into each other, and Paul starts his moaning, but it doesn't seem to help—he looks green in the face. Uncle Johan and Birger stand upright as if they were on land, and they don't even notice how badly the boat is rocking.

The salmon net is spread out over a length of about fifty yards. Hundreds of cork disks are tied to the outside, all around, to keep the net afloat. Uncle Johan and Birger grip the net and pull the boat slowly along around it. From time to time they kneel down, lean far out, and look into the water.

"There is one!" Birger cries, and Uncle Johan hauls a bit of the net up. A big salmon struggles in the mesh, and Uncle Johan takes it out and slaps it hard against the board. This kills the salmon at once. Then he tosses it over to us.

"What's the weight?" he asks. I pick it up. It has a bluish sheen, and its belly is silvery, and it is *very* heavy. "Twenty-five pounds," I answer.

"Not quite," Birger says, and looks at the fish, "but a good eighteen pounds, I guess."

One more salmon is found in the net, this time a smaller one.

"Why do only salmon get caught in your net?" asks Paul.

"Haven't you seen the glass buoys in the water?" Uncle Johan says. "They are attached to the net, and on them I have written with indelible ink: *Inngang laks bare!*—Entrance for salmon only!"

"Ha-ha!" says Paul, but we all laugh; it's a good joke, really.

"All right, Vikings, here is the real story," says Uncle Johan now. "The salmon swim high in the water, only a few feet beneath the surface. So to catch salmon I put our net high in the water. That's the whole secret.

"Flounders, for instance, keep to the bottom of shallow water. Herring, again, go into deep water. You never find a herring or a flounder in a salmon net, and never a salmon among a herring catch. The different kinds of fish live on different water levels.

"And now to work, Vikings!"

It's Friday today, and every Friday afternoon the salmon nets must be taken out and brought into the harbor. There they stay till Monday afternoon. This is a law in Norway, and because of the three days' rest, the salmon never dies out in our waters.

All four of us haul the big net up. I pull and pull at the wet, slippery ropes. It is very hard work, because big stones are fastened to them to hold the net down, and every single stone has to be heaved aboard, and the whole net too. Yard by yard we haul it in—my arms hurt from pulling and heaving. It takes us almost an hour to get the net into the boat. The sweat runs down my face. I do not even feel the rough sea any longer, and Paul makes a face at me. I know what he means: "We asked for it, and now we've got it!"

At last the salmon net and the stones are in the boat, and we settle back in our corner and suddenly feel very cold and tired. Birger takes a cord from his pocket, winds it around the starter wheel of the motor, and pulls sharp: that makes the motor start up with a tokka-tokka-tokka, and back we speed at last.

"Uncle Johan," I ask, "how come all the salmon are so big when you catch them? Aren't there ever any small ones? Where are they when they are young?"

"Don't you know the life story of the salmon?" Birger asks back. "There are no young salmon in the ocean."

"They are not *born* old, are they?" says Paul.

"No, Flinky. They are not. They are born young, like you and me. But they are born far up the rivers, and there the salmon stay till they are two or three years old. Only then do they migrate down the rivers and out into the great ocean. There the salmon stay, if they are not caught.

"In the salt water, they grow very fast. But one day they start travelling again, and they migrate from wherever they are in the big ocean right back to the fresh-water rivers from which they swam out into the sea years ago. And then the salmon do something strange. They swim up the river, back to the waters where they were born. There they lay their many thousands of tiny eggs, and soon after that they die."

"What about the rapids and waterfalls in the rivers? We can go shooting the rapids down the river, but we couldn't do it upstream, against the current!"

"No, we can't, of course not. But the salmon can. It sounds incredible, but it is quite true, boys. A salmon can jump the rapids against the current, in tremendous leaps several times its own length."

We are soon back at the boathouse, and taking the two salmon inside. Birger weighs them. "Eighteen pounds," he says, "just as I told you! And the second one is fifteen pounds. That was a good catch."

Ingvald Runde packs the salmon into ice for the night. Tomorrow he will send them all off to Aalesund.

Outside Uncle Johan's old boathouse stands a huge stone tank with copper-sulphate solution. All four of us drag the salmon net over the pier to the tank and dump it in. Here it will soak for twenty-four hours. The solution keeps the net from rotting. After soaking, the net is spread on the breakwater wall to dry, and there the holes are mended, too. On Monday afternoon the nets are taken out to sea, and then they stay another four days in the water.

Paul and I take the cork disks off the net and take them to the old boathouse. Uncle Johan sits on an overturned boat cutting lengths from a ten-pound ball of string; he needs them for mending the net tomorrow.

"Herre Runde, why don't you build a new boathouse? This one is really falling apart," Paul says.

"True enough, it's falling apart," Uncle Johan says. "I really should build a new one. But it is the oldest house on the island, and it has a story.

"It happened eighty years ago, on a Sunday.

"My grandparents lived in this house. It stood away from the other houses, down on the beach here. That Sunday, all the people from the village had rowed over to Heroey Island to church. Only two persons stayed behind—my grandmother, and my father, who was just one month old.

"My grandmother told me how it all happened. She went outside to look after the cow. Suddenly she saw flames farther up in the village. Grandmother went inside, took her baby in her arms, and ran to the burning house. She opened the stable door and chased the horse and the cow outside. That was all she could do.

"The wind was driving the sparks toward the next houses, which stood close together at that time. Grandmother went there, and again she opened the door to the stable and to the pigsty, and chased the animals out and away from the fire. She ran from house to house, always with her baby in her arms, and everywhere she let the animals out and drove them up the slopes.

"There were about twenty houses here at that time, and the strong wind carried the flames from one house to the next till they all went

up in flames. All except ours—and that was saved only because it stood more than two hundred yards away from the others. The sparks didn't fly as far as that.

"Grandmother looked on and cried. She couldn't do anything more, and at least she had saved all the animals.

"The villagers saw the fire from Heroey Island and rowed back as fast as they could, and people came from many other islands to help. But it was too late.

"That night, about seventy people slept in this old house here, and next morning they started rebuilding the village. They decided that never again would they build their houses so close together.

"When I grew up, I built my own house up there, away from the beach. But I never rebuilt this one, and I never will. I think I shall let it stand as it was eighty years ago, till it falls down by itself.

"And now off with you, Vikings, and thanks for helping me with the nets. *God kveld!*"

"Thank you for taking us along, and *god kveld!*" we say, and walk home.

It must be almost midnight, but it is still light. Farther north, above the Arctic Circle, the sun never sets during these summer weeks. Here at Runde Island it does, but only for a few hours, and even then it never gets really dark. I can read without lights at midnight.

Father and Mother and Aase are still up. I say good night, and go up to my room.

I move my pillow to the other side of my bed, so that the light from the window falls on my book. I like to read in my bird book before I fall asleep. But I cannot read long tonight. I think of the fire on the island, and nobody there to help Uncle Johan's grandmother, and how courageous she was. She was only nineteen years old when it happened.

I turn around and look up to the sky. My wild goose swings slowly before my eyes in the night wind. I made it from odds and ends of cloth and stuffed it with hay.

Back and forth it swings, and forth and back—and I fall asleep.

"Jarle! The *Sigurd* is coming in, don't you hear the ship's horn, you sleepy-fish? Father is leaving, and you've already missed *frokost!*"

Aase is calling me. I jump out of bed and into my pants. "No time for washing now," I say to myself, "but never mind." I slip into my pullover and slide down the banister.

With Father carrying the bundle with his tools, and me carrying his suitcase, we all walk together to the pier.

We shake hands, and Father kisses little Trygve, and then he walks up the gangplank. Ingvald Runde comes with his truck and brings the salmon catch—two crates today!

Captain Andersen waves to me from the bridge, and then he gives a signal to the crewmen. The ropes are loosened and thrown on board, and the *Sigurd* is off. Father is leaning against the railing, and we wave to each other till the boat disappears in the morning mist.

After breakfast we start haying, and Aase and I hang the hay on the wires.

The sun is out, and everybody is working in the fields. Hay is all we get from our fields, and we need it for the horses and cows. We harvest it twice each year: once in summer, and then again in fall.

Our little field borders on Uncle Johan's. Cousin Ingebjoerg waves to me to come over. I make a sign that I must first finish hanging the hay. But Mother says, "Go right over, Jarle. Ingebjoerg began asking for you as early as six o'clock this morning, but we couldn't get you awake then, you were fast asleep.

"They went up the *fjells* this morning and wanted you to help them find some sheep. We are almost finished with our hay, anyway."

I go over to Ingebjoerg. The horse Fritjof is just pulling the hay wagon up the ramp and into the barn, and Uncle Johan is pushing from the rear. I like Fritjof much better when he is not working, without that bridle and halter. He doesn't look beautiful at all today, pulling the cart.

"Jarle, Einar Runde saw four of our sheep near his forest in the *fjells* yesterday. Hans-Jakob and I went up this morning and found three. We brought them down for shearing, but Bruse is still missing. Can you go up with us and help me look for it? Father and Mother are busy; they want to hay while the sun is shining."

34

So it's Bruse again. It has already missed one shearing, and must have a long coat by now, if it is still alive. Uncle Johan has twenty sheep, twelve Norwegian and eight Scottish ones. The Scottish sheep they keep on the fenced-in hills behind their house. But the Norwegian sheep graze all over the *fjells* of the island. They roam around freely with the other islanders' sheep, and look for food even on the dangerous cliffs and in the precipices. They are stronger and more sure-footed than the Scottish sheep, but they are hard to find when you want them for the shearing. Every year some of them fall to their death over the cliffs. It can't be helped; there isn't enough **grass**land for all the sheep on the fenced-in slopes.

Ingebjoerg signals to Hans-Jakob, who is helping his mother load hay onto the cart, and he comes along. Together we climb up the *fjells*. It is very rocky here, and there are many plants growing be-

tween the stones. We are used to climbing, and we go up as fast as down. We leap from rock to rock till we are high up on the mountain. From here we have a good view of the *fjells.*

"I hope Bruse is still alive," says Ingebjoerg. "Two of our sheep have already fallen from the cliffs this year."

"Maybe she's hiding between the rocks around the puffin caves," I say, because I know there is good grass up there, and I have noticed that sheep often graze there.

There she stands, that stupid old sheep, right at the entrance to the cave, with her stupid ears turned up, and looking surprised. We chase her down the *fjells* and right into the enclosure behind Uncle Johan's house.

Aunt Kari is there, shearing the other sheep. Hans-Jakob's grandmother is helping her.

"We found Bruse," Hans-Jakob shouts.

"I am awfully glad you helped us, Jarle," says Aunt Kari. "We had given her up. You know what? I am going to knit you a beautiful pullover from Bruse's wool!"

Ingebjoerg holds Bruse's head, and Aunt Kari clips off the heavy fleece. Aunt Kari and my cousins comb and spin and dye the wool afterwards, with no outside help.

Teacher Mikklebust is kneeling in the grass.

"*God morgen,* Jarle," he says. "Here, hold it carefully," and he passes a very small gull from his closed hands into mine. "I found it in its nest."

Teacher Mikklebust has a string of bird rings hanging around his neck. There are many different sizes: very small, small, medium, large, and extra large, for the various sizes of birds. They are made of aluminum, because the birds couldn't fly with a heavy band around a leg.

On each band is a number, and the address: STAVANGER MUSEUM, STAVANGER, NORWAY. Teacher Per chooses the smallest ring from his necklace and bends it open. He slips it around one leg of the little gull, and tightens it a bit with his pliers, but not too tight, so it will not harm the leg even when the gull's legs have grown.

"Why do you put the ring on such a small bird?" I ask. "It can't fly very far yet."

"It will be able to, soon," Teacher Per answers. "Only last winter my friends at the Stavanger Museum sent me a letter they got. It said, 'Number 2467 found dead December 2, east coast of New-foundland.' I took my notebook and checked up, and there was my entry: 'No. 2467. Sea gull, about three weeks old, ringed July 12.' So the little sea gull had gone on migration with a flight of older birds when it was not older than four months, and it travelled all the way from Norway to Newfoundland with them, right across the ocean."

Bird watchers all over the world know about bird banding. When they find a band on a bird's leg, they always look for the address on it and return the ring there. This is the way in which one finds out about the places to which the birds migrate, how long it takes them to get there, where they stop on their flights, and even how long they live. Teacher Per explained it all to us in school, long before he took us along to help him.

A big gull shrieks above us in the air. She circles and circles, and suddenly she swoops down on us, barely missing our heads, then soars away again. We dodge, of course, and Teacher Per laughs.

"That was the mother gull, trying to scare us away from her young one. She doesn't know we don't mean any harm."

Again the mother gull dives at us with angry screeches. "Kitty-veek," she cries, "kitty-veek, kitty-veek." The little gull feels warm and soft in my hands, and so fragile—I can feel the tiny bones in its body. It doesn't bite or scratch, like bigger ones. Teacher Per has cuts and scratches from them all over his hands.

The ring is on the foot now, with name and address and number. Now that it is banded, I put the gull carefully back into its nest.

"Let's try to catch puffins, Jarle," says Teacher Per. "I brought the net along. Maybe we'll find some in a rabbit's burrow."

"I've already seen a few this morning," I tell him, "when we were looking for sheep. I think they flew up from a rabbit's burrow in a cave." And I lead him to the place where I found Bruse.

"That would be fine," Teacher Per says. "I haven't had much luck lately with those lazy invaders."

"Why lazy invaders?" I ask.

"You saw them flying out of a rabbit's hole this morning, Jarle, didn't you?"

"Yes, I did."

"And how did they get in?"

"I never thought of that."

"I'll tell you. The puffins come to our island in spring for nesting. But many of them are too lazy to build their own nests. Now, the rabbits build comfortable little living holes down below in the ground—their living rooms, really. The puffins get together in commando groups of ten or even twenty, and they chase the rabbits out of their burrows, take over the holes, and make themselves comfortable in their conquered living rooms."

We are near the caves now, and lie down on our bellies, watching quietly.

"I can hear them!" Teacher Per whispers.

40

"Orr orr orr!" There they are! First I hear them, and then I see one right on the rock before us. It shakes its yellow hook-bill and looks around.

"Orr orr orr," it goes, and two more come up and sit next to it.

Regardez! Voilà les puffins! Look, there are the puffins!" I hear an excited voice. I turn around. Farther down, Paul is standing with François, and pointing up.

"Hush! Get down!" we whisper, and they throw themselves to the ground. Paul must have gone looking for us, and when he didn't find us at Long Point he brought François along. François is a French boy who is spending his summer vacation with Uncle Jakob and Aunt Jorun. We have taught him some Norwegian, but when he is excited he speaks French. And I have learned a few words of his language.

The birds haven't noticed us yet. They look funny with their huge colored beaks, and their white-and-black suits and red feet.

Teacher Per creeps up to the rock and throws his net toward the puffins and over the rabbit hole under the rock.

All three puffins on the rock have escaped and flown off. But two more were sitting on the ground, and those we get.

"Orr orr orr," they rattle. When we take them carefully from the net, they look at us as if they were astonished and not at all angry, and they don't fight when Teacher Per puts the bands on their feet.

"Look at the tremendous beaks!" François exclaims.

"They certainly need them," says Teacher Per. "They fly out to sea and dive for fish, and they can store six fish crosswise in their roomy beaks before they fly home again to the nest and feed their young ones with the catch."

"Why do they store them crosswise?" François wants to know.

"If they put them lengthwise in their beaks, the fish would slide down their throats, I suppose," Paul answers, "and nothing would be left for the young ones."

"Correct," says Teacher Per. "And when the young ones are old enough to go out fishing by themselves, the beak of the parent puffin shrinks. The storeroom disappears till next spring, when the puffins have young ones again."

"That's very practical," says Paul, "a storeroom that disappears when one doesn't need it. *Very* practical."

"*Incroyable!*" François exclaims in French, which means "incredible."

"It's true," Teacher Per answers, "and there are more incredible facts about the puffins. They help each other, whenever one of them is in need. If a puffin parent dies, for instance, another one takes care of the young one, and teaches it how to fly and how to swim and how to catch fish."

After the puffins are banded, we let them fly off, and Teacher Per puts his net into his bag. He is in a very happy mood. He has banded almost two thousand birds this summer, but very few of them were puffins.

We walk down the slopes now, and keep looking for birds. Teacher Per spots more than we three others together. We catch four more gulls, one raven, and three oyster catchers.

"Look, sea gull eggs!" Paul cries. There they lie in their nest, and we get down and study them carefully, but we do not touch the grass around, or the nest itself. The mother gull might not come back

to hatch them if she found the nest disturbed. We wait a long time for the mother sea gull. But no bird comes back to the nest.

"May we take the eggs to the club for our collection?" I ask Teacher Per.

He lies down and studies the nest carefully.

"Yes, you may," he says. "Look at the grass around the eggs. It hasn't been touched for days. The eggs have been abandoned by the bird, because no young ones will come out of these, and the bird knew it and didn't come back."

We take only abandoned eggs for our collection, never one that may be hatched. I take one egg, and François carries the second one. Teacher Per says:

"You go ahead and take the eggs to your bird club. I am going back to the *fjells*. Perhaps I can catch a black-coat gull. I saw a few circling around up there yesterday, chasing puffins, I think."

François and I carry our eggs very carefully down the slope, but Paul races down.

"A big sea gull!" he shouts to us, "I've caught a big sea gull!" and he throws his hands around the wings of a bird. But then he jumps up and moves back in disgust.

"Phew! It's a dead one!" he hollers, and holds his stomach.

"You are a fine bird collector!" I say. "Why don't you invite a live gull to visit us and let us study her in our club?" But Paul refuses to touch the dead bird, and so he takes the egg from François, and François lugs the heavy, big sea gull to our club.

We come down, cross the road, and walk among the boulders to our bird club. This is a hut that was put up as a tool shed when the island road was built, but nobody used it after that, and Hans-Jakob had the idea of cleaning it up and turning it into our clubhouse. There we meet and bring all the eggs and feathers and dead birds we find.

We decided to call ourselves the Hubro Club, which means Club of the Eagle Owl. Over the entrance I painted an owl sitting on a branch, and above it the word HUBRO. Our club is more than a year old, and only boys belong to it.

The door is open, which means that Hans-Jakob is there. He is the president, and only he has a key to the club. He and Olav are sitting at the desk busily plucking feathers from a wing. We show them the eggs we found, and the big sea gull, and together we decide to make a display of its black feathers. But first we measure the length of our big gull, and the width of the outspread wings, and check in our books: it *is* a real black-coat gull! There are not more than twenty of them on our island, and they live so high up on the cliffs of Bird Mountain that they have almost never been caught alive. We must tell Teacher Per about our find.

"Look what I found this morning!" Olav says, and he shows us *his* find.

"Razor-billed auk!" I say. "How did you get a razor-billed auk egg?"

"Don't break your tongue, Jarle," Olav answers. "First tell me how you know it *is* from an auk."

"Look at the shape, Olav," I tell him. "Do you see how pointed it is at one end? There's a long description in my bird book, which says that auks don't build nests, they lay their eggs right on the bare rocks, even on the ledges of the cliffs. Because of its odd shape, the egg doesn't roll off the cliff when the wind blows—it just spins around in a circle."

"I don't believe it," says Olav.

"I'll show you," says Hans-Jakob. He puts the egg on the table and we blow from one side. The egg turns around and around—but it doesn't roll off the table.

"That's neat construction," Paul says. "If ever I invent a new balloon to keep steady in the wind, I would use the shape of that egg."

"Wonderful invention," says Hans-Jakob, "except it was invented a long time ago. In America they call it a blimp."

All the members of our club have come in by now. We are nine boys, and we work on our nest displays and on our feather collections. Jan smears some whitish stuff on the bird rock he is building; it is a rock with nests on it and sea gull eggs in the nests. The white stuff smells horrible.

"What is it?" I ask Jan.

"Nature's glue," Jan answers. "I scraped it off the cliffs myself. Real fine sea gull droppings. It *looks* natural too, doesn't it!"

We have fits of laughter.

"I don't care whether it looks natural," I say, "but it *smells* natural. Open the door!"

Outside stand Halvard and little Leif, his brother, and they smile shyly at me. They are dressed in their fishing outfits and are carrying a big wooden ship's model in their arms.

"The herring fleet is coming!" I call to the others, and everybody squeezes into the entrance to see what's going on.

Halvard and Leif still don't say anything, so Hans-Jakob asks them what they want.

"We want to join the Hubro Club," says Halvard, "and we have brought you our model boat, as a present, if you will let us join."

"We would like to have you in our club, even without the boat as a present, but we have those rules, you know. Isn't that so, Hans-Jakob? Tell them, you are the president!" I say.

"Yes, those rules," says Hans-Jakob. "Rule number two of our club says that, inasmuch as going after bird nests and birds in the wild *fjells* is a dangerous occupation, and inasmuch as otherwise parents would make life miserable for us, no boy

below the age of twelve can be accepted as a member of the bird club, otherwise called Hubro Club."

"See! I told you!" I say to Halvard and Leif. "How about starting your own club? Halvard could be president, and Leif, you'd make a very good vice president. We will help you find a place in a boathouse, and all the boys who have models will join you."

Halvard and Leif like the idea, and I promise to paint a club sign on their door, a Viking boat. And now we invite them to visit our club, and show them everything.

"I have to leave," Hans-Jakob says. "My father wants me to help mend the nets. Jan, will you take care of the keys, and give them back to me in the afternoon?"

Together we go to the breakwater. Uncle Johan is sitting on the stone wall, where his big salmon net is spread out to dry, and is mending the holes in it. He uses a wooden bobbin, with a piece of string through its eye.

Every Friday, when the net is hauled in from the sea, there are new holes in it, and if they are not found and mended at once the salmon caught in the net next week will escape. They are very good at finding holes, and getting into free waters again.

Uncle Johan teaches Hans-Jakob how to use the lengths of string with the wooden bobbin, and how to make the right knots, and how not to draw the holes together too tight or too wide. I look on for a while, but then it gets boring, so I say *"God dag"* and go back to my bicycle and ride home.

I pass Einar Runde's boathouse. The roof is thick with grass, and many flowers are growing in it. In former times, almost every house had a sod roof, but now most roofs are covered with slate tiles from the mainland. Einar Runde has kept his sod roof, and even poppies—which grow nowhere else on the island—grow up there. He brought the seed back from the shores of the Sea of Galilee, in the Holy Land, where he went on a pilgrimage many years ago.

As long as the poppies are blooming, Einar Runde never cuts the grass on his roof. The high grass shelters the poppies from the wind, and they grow better that way.

Ingrid Runde comes out of the house. She is Einar Runde's daughter, and the second teacher we have on the island. Most people on Runde Island have the name Runde, so we call everybody by the first name too. Ingrid Runde teaches the lower grades, and singing and knitting in all grades. We have known each other for many years. We

were good friends long before she became a teacher. Ingrid is carrying a big milk can on her shoulders; she is on her way to the meadow, where her family keeps two cows.

"*God dag*, Ingrid!" I say and pass her on my bicycle.

"Jarle," she calls after me, "wait for me!"

I stop and wait for her to catch up. She looks at me and then, before I even know what she is doing, she quickly stretches out her hand and twists my nose.

"Hey, let go!" I shout.

I really think she has gone nuts. Ingrid laughs and says, "But you asked for it!" And from my back she rips a piece of paper that had been pinned to my pullover by somebody. On the paper is written in big letters:

PLEASE TWIST MY NOSE!

So that is it. One of my treacherous friends at the bird club must have played that dirty trick on me. I bet it was Hans-Jakob, when I opened the door. I will get my revenge!

I jump on my bicycle and race off. When I get to Ingvald Runde's Landhandel, I stop. The store window has changed since this morning. The *Sigurd* has brought the new goods for the fishermen, and Ingvald Runde has made a beautiful display of them.

Huge balls of string and cord in many sizes hang in the window. New nets are spread out, and ropes of every length and thickness. Cork disks and orange-colored glass buoys decorate the nets, and there are straw-covered water bottles. The fishermen take hot coffee along in them in wintertime. And hundreds and hundreds of fishhooks are on display. I wish I could buy a whole collection of them.

"François was here," says Mother. "He is waiting for you at Uncle Jakob's. Take your oilskin along, they're going fishing." But first we eat dinner—fish soup and fish pudding.

50

Uncle Jakob lives at the other end of the road, in one of the last houses on the island. He is still making hay, because the sun has been shining for hours and hours, and there was no fog all day long. We've been very lucky today.

"Coming to help me, Jarle?" Uncle Jakob asks. "That's nice of you. I am almost finished. Aunt Jorun has already gone in with Paul and François, you can join them and have some of the salmon we smoked yesterday." But I stay with Uncle Jakob. We always have good talks when we are together; he knows so much about the sea.

Uncle Jakob has a very fast fishing cutter with a twelve-man crew, and he has promised to take me on his ship as a deck hand, as soon as my school years are over. He is the best skipper around, everybody knows that, and so everybody wants to join his crew when he goes out with the herring fleet in winter, or codfishing up north. He works the crew hard, but he himself works even harder.

This past spring he came home from the Lofoten islands, up above the Arctic Circle, with the biggest catch of his life. Twenty thousand

fishermen had gone there in two thousand vessels from all along the coast and all the islands of Norway. Every evening they had put out their lines, each a mile or more long, and with about fifteen hundred hooks hanging down from it. In the mornings, they take the lines in, and on most of the hooks hangs a cod-fish. They work all day long with short lines, too. This season the sea was packed with fish, which had come in shoals more than a hundred feet wide.

"Why aren't you out with your ship, Uncle Jakob?" I ask.

"Well, Jarle, everything has its time. There is a time for herring fishing, there is a time for the codfish, and there is a time to go seal hunting. But now is the time for haying. I can't let my bit of grassland go unused. And meanwhile, my friend Gunnar has gone to Iceland with my fishing vessel."

"To Iceland! I wish I were on your ship right now, Uncle."

"I know you would like going up north—you always wanted to be-come an explorer, Jarle. But as I said, everything has its time. Let's go in, now that we have all the hay up, or the other boys won't have left a bite for you!"

"Get into your oilskins," Uncle Jakob says, after he has finished his coffee, "and let's go down to the boat."

"*Godt fiske!*" Aunt Jorun wishes us, and we walk to the beach.

We push the boat into the water, and Uncle Jakob takes the oars. With a few strokes, the boat is out on the sea. The water is calm and clear; I can see the bottom. The rocks down there are covered with green and brown algae and moss, which float and sway back and forth. Hundreds of small fish swim around, and a few circular jellyfish float on the surface like transparent whitish saucers.

I don't touch them, because they sting your hands, but Uncle Jakob doesn't mind that: he reaches into the water and grabs one, and in his hand it loses its form and becomes only a lump of jelly.

We throw the fishing lines out. A minute later I feel a weight on mine, and something jerks at it. I pull the line in, quickly and with a steady draw, and a big mackerel is hanging on it.

François's first catch is a flounder, and Paul has a coalfish on the hook. Uncle Jakob lets us do all the fishing. It is only when we lose a fish or when we don't handle the bait and the line right that he lends us a helping hand.

The sun goes down behind Bird Mountain, but it stays light. We have caught three mackerels and seven flounders and nine coalfish.

"Time to get home," says Uncle Jakob.

On the way back, it is our turn to row. Uncle Jakob stands in the stern and throws the line out. He handles it with quick pulls, as if he wanted to tease the fish with the bait. And really, he does catch another two mackerels and three more coalfish—polefish as we call them when they are young ones.

By the time we are back it is long past ten o'clock. We pull the boat along the rocky beach into a small inlet, and tie it to a pole.

Paul and François carry one box with the catch up to the house, while Uncle Jakob carries the second one.

Aunt Jorun is standing in the cellar door. "Bring them right in," she says. "How many did you catch?"

"I had able helpers today," Uncle Jakob answers. "We caught twenty-four fish. Let's cook the polefish and have a good midnight meal; they taste best the night they are caught."

We help clean the fish, and Aunt Jorun boils all twelve of them in onion water. We sit in the kitchen and talk till the fish is ready; this takes half an hour on the electric stove. Then we each eat two fish, which are wonderful. François says, *"Délicieux! Incroyable!"* and he eats four fish all by himself.

Paul and I each get two mackerels to take home, and then it's twelve o'clock, and we say *"Tusen takk"* and walk home.

I tiptoe into the kitchen and fill a bucket with water for the two mackerels I brought home. Then I go up to my room and straight to sleep—I am too tired even to read.

Mother knocks on the kitchen ceiling with the end of her broomstick, and I hear it through the floor of my room.

"*Vaagn opp,* Jarle!" I hear her voice. "Wake up! It's St. Olav's Day!"

Why should I get up so early, I wonder. It's Sunday, can't I sleep a bit longer today? But then I see on my watch that it's past nine o'clock, and I jump out of bed and slide down the banister and go to the bathroom in the cellar.

The electric water heater is on, and I draw some hot water. The second switch starts the electric room heater. We have a lot of electricity in Norway, because of the thousands of rivers and waterfalls

all over the country. They drive the turbines, and the turbines produce electricity. It comes to our island from the mainland through cables on the bottom of the sea.

After my bath, I have breakfast and run over to Uncle Johan's. Cousin Marit is standing at the door, all dressed up and looking into the sky. Her brooch with the two little silver shoes is dangling on her blouse, and as she blows the hair away from her face she calls "Kitty-veek! Kitty-veek!"

"Are you a bird," I ask, "or what ails you?"

"I am not a bird, and don't be so silly," she answers. "Can't you see I am in my best dress? I'm going to Heroey Island with Teacher Ingrid, and I'm going to be a bridesmaid, because Ingrid's cousin is getting married today."

"I didn't say you are not in your best dress. All I want to know is why you are screeching like a sea gull!"

"I wasn't screeching, I was calling a sea gull—there she is again! Move away, Jarle, or she won't come near, and then . . ."

"And then what?" I ask.

"Promise not to tell!"

"I promise."

"And then my wish wouldn't come true! If you call a sea gull from your doorstep, and the sea gull comes, it brings good luck and your wish comes true, but you mustn't tell anybody what your wish is!"

"And what *is* your wish, Marit?"

"Can you keep a secret, Jarle?"

"Of course!"

"So can I! Look, there she is again! Kitty-veek! Kitty-veek!" Marit screeches again at the top of her voice. And really, I do see sea gulls flying low, and one circling above us.

"Kitty-veek," the sea gull calls, and "Kitty-veek," Marit calls back.

"When is the boat going over to Heroey for the wedding?" Aunt Kari asks, but nobody knows. All the weddings in our district are held in the big church on Heroey Island, and all Christmas and Easter services too.

Our minister serves five islands, and he goes to each island seven times a year in his own motorboat. When he comes to our island, he holds service in our new Community Hall. We all belong to the Evangelical Lutheran Church, which is the national church of our country.

"Hans-Jakob," Aunt Kari says, "run over to Einar Runde's. He is taking the girls to Heroey Island in his motorboat. Ask him when Marit should be there." Of course, I go along with my cousin.

Teacher Ingrid is standing with three friends in front of her house. They are all decked out in the festive dress of our district. Their skirts and blouses are embroidered with red and green and brown leaves and flowers, and they are wearing the same kind of silver brooch as Marit. Ingrid is helping Liv fasten hers. She tells us that the boat will leave at one o'clock.

On the way we meet Mother and my sisters and Trygve, all on their way to Uncle Johan's for the family dinner, and we greet each other with *"God Olav's dag!"*

On this day, people all over Norway eat our national dish, the *roemmegroet*. We eat it three times a year: on May 17th, because this is the day of Norway's Independence; then we eat it on Harvest Day, and again on St. Olav's Day.

Today there are fourteen of us around the table in Uncle Johan's house. In the middle stands our flag. Hans-Jakob says the prayer, and then we sit down and dig into the *roemmegroet*. It is made of milk and cream and rice, with sliced hard-boiled eggs on top, and sprinkled with raisins and sugar and cinnamon. Just before we eat it, Aunt Kari pours hot melted butter over it, till the *roemmegroet* swims in a yellow pool.

We drink buttermilk with it, and it takes me a long time to finish my plate: *roemmegroet* is always much more than it looks.

After the meal, Hans-Jakob's grandmother sits down at her harmonium, and Uncle Johan takes out his violin, and I the guitar. First we play hymns and sing. Then Uncle Johan plays a sonata by Edvard Grieg on his violin. It is a bit sad, and Grandmother says:

"Johan and Jarle, play me an old Ole Bull dance," and for that we do not need any score. Ole Bull was a famous violinist, but he also wrote songs and dance tunes when Grandmother was a young girl, and they are played even now. It is getting gay, and the girls dance around and we sing and play. But then Grandmother gives a signal on her harmonium, playing three long-drawn-out notes, and says:

"That was very nice, thank you, Johan and Jarle. And now let us sing our National Anthem." We all sing *"Ja, vi elsker dette landet."*

> Yes, we love with fond devotion
> This our land that looms
> Rugged, storm-scarred, over the ocean
> With her thousand homes.

Uncle Johan is pasting pictures in his album, and we crowd around him. Cousin Liv and Hans-Jakob look on from one side, and Ingebjoerg and I from the other. Uncle Johan shows us a new photograph, a picture of herring fishers.

"Can you recognize me?" he asks. "The big rope is just above my head. The photo was taken last winter, when we had that big catch. You can see it, the net was bulging with herring, it was quite a job to hold on to it. You know we tie our boats together, and then every man in the boats grips the net and we haul it up. That time it was almost too heavy with fish, and we were afraid the net might break. It had happened before, three years ago. We lost the entire herring catch that time, and we lost the valuable net too.

"Well, this time the net held, but our hands were bleeding from the rough ropes and the heavy pull."

"But how did you get the photograph?" I ask. "And who took it?"

"A newspaper in Oslo had sent a photographer because they had heard that we expected a very big catch. He came alongside in his motorboat and took pictures. Do you know where I saw it? In a calendar, over on Heroey Island, last week, when I went to the meeting of our district council. So I wrote to the photographer, and he sent me the picture."

"I remember a poem about herring fishing, and about sea gulls," says Hans-Jakob. "I think I read it in a book once, with 'Ho, let's go! Ho, let's go!'"

"What book did you read it in, Hans-Jakob?" Ingebjoerg asks.

"I don't remember," Hans-Jakob says, but we others wink at each other and Ingebjoerg says:

"You don't remember, because you didn't read it in a book at all. I taught you the poem, and Jarle was here too. Am I right, Jarle?" Ingebjoerg is right, and Uncle Johan says, "If you all remember the poem, why don't you say it now?" So we say it together:

> "Now it is lively, and much to be done.
>   Ho, let's go! Ho, let's go!
>   The herring is coming, goes toward land.
>   Ho, let's go! Ho, let's go!
>   Whales are a-tumbling about the horizon.
>   The porpoise frolics and the coalfish leaps,
>   While the sea-swallow cries her hungry cry.
>   Ho, let's go!
>
> "Now it is lively, and much to be done.
>   Ho, let's go! Ho, let's go!
>   The sea birds are chatting away today.
>   Ho, let's go! Ho, let's go!
>   It sounds like women at a coffee party.
>   The gray gull shrieks and the white gull moans,
>   While a third one steals their fish away.
>   Ho, let's go!
>
> Now it is lively, and much to be done.
>   Ho, let's go! Ho, let's go!
>   The fishermen cry, 'Haul up the net!'
>   Ho, let's go! Ho, let's go!
>   It rises up, and look how quick
>   The sea is alive with millions of herring
>   And the sun is darkened by thousands of wings!
>   Ho, let's go! Ho, let's go!"

"That's a very true poem," Uncle Johan says.

I leaf through the album. On one of the picture post cards I see a mountain rising from the sea, with a hole going right through it, and I ask Uncle Johan about it.

"It is the peak of Torghatten. You can see it is shaped like an old hat, with a hole through it. Look at the next picture, Jarle, that's a rock right on the Arctic Circle, the Hestmannoey. This Horseman rock and the Torghatten are quite near each other, I always pass them on my way up to the Lofoten islands, and I bought these two picture post cards last year.

"According to an old Norse legend, the Hestmannoey was a great horseman in olden times. He wanted to marry the daughter of the mighty Soemna King; her name was Lekamoey. But she made fun of him, and one day the Horseman shot an arrow at her.

"The mighty Soemna King saw it, and he threw his giant hat down, in the path of the whirring arrow. The arrow passed right through the hat, but its power was broken, and Lekamoey was saved.

"That very moment the sun rose up over the horizon, and the Horseman and the King and the Princess Lekamoey, and even the hat, turned into stone. And ever since, the four of them have been standing there and looking at each other."

Uncle Johan closes his album.

"That's enough for today," he says. "I'll show you more pictures some other time."

64

Ingebjoerg and Liv sit down with their knitting, and chat. They work on their new pullovers from our homespun wool. I take a book from the shelf, a history of the Second World War, by Sir Winston Churchill, who was the Prime Minister of Great Britain at that time. Uncle bought it after he had made that good herring catch last winter. There are nine volumes, with many illustrations, bound in white leather and with gold lettering on the spine.

One of the volumes tells the story of the naval battles in the *fjords* of Norway, and how the Norwegians helped the British to fight the enemy. I read for a long time. Hans-Jakob reads too. His book is *A Happy Boy,* by Bjoernstjerne Bjoernson, the poet who wrote the words for our National Anthem.

Afterwards, Hans-Jakob and I go down to the beach. It's a very clear day, and the hay on the wires is drying well.

"Look," says Hans-Jakob, "it's so clear I can count every tree in Einar Runde's forest."

When Einar Runde came back from the Holy Land many years ago, he planted that forest on the rocky slopes behind his house. He said that's how he had seen it done on the slopes of the Valley of Jezreel. Father told me that the people on our island thought Einar Runde very stupid at that time, and they refused to help him, because the trees would never grow on the rocky ground. Who had ever heard of planting trees on bare mountains? they said.

But Einar Runde did not give in. He told the school children how he had seen it done with his own eyes, and all the children of Runde came and helped him plant the saplings that he had brought to the island. And now everybody wished he had done the same—we would have trees all over the mountainside.

The forest protects the fields from the wind, and that's why Einar Runde's fields are the best ones on the island. Every year he sells a few trees for Christmas, and for making hay poles. But he doesn't like to sell many. He says a tree is cut down in an hour, but it takes years to grow, and he always plants new trees to replace the ones he cuts down.

Paul comes running toward us.

"Quick!" he shouts from afar. "The pilot boat's going to the light-house. Chief Pilot Monsen is taking us along!"

We race down to the harbor and up the gangplank to the pilot boat. Pilot Oestensen is there too. He got a message to bring spare parts for the Diesel engine in the lighthouse.

The pilot boat is always kept in readiness. Whenever a big ship comes in from the ocean on her way to Aalesund, the chief pilot gets a wireless message, and then he or Pilot Oestensen goes out and meets the ship and guides her safely through the dangerous waters.

We pass along the coast of our island and are heading west toward Bird Mountain and the lighthouse. All of a sudden, a wall of fog creeps down over the mountain, and after a few minutes our island has disappeared. The foghorn starts its warning signals, and the boat cuts her speed.

"If the fog stays like that, we won't see a bird!" Paul says.

"It won't stay," answers Pilot Oestensen. "There's a westerly wind, and we are heading right into it. That wind drives the fog in another direction, we should be through it soon, and then we will have sunshine again."

The fog gets thinner, and I can make out Cormorant Rock.

"Look at the showoffs," says Pilot Oestensen. "They always sit on top of the rocks because they want to be seen, those vain birds."

"And they are greedy like anything," I tell Pilot Oestensen. "Last month Uncle Johan found a dead cormorant floating in the water. He brought it home for our bird club, and there were forty-seven little fish in his stomach."

We steer close to the rock. Now I see a whole family of razor-billed auks standing there behind the cormorants. With their white breasts and black heads and coats, they look like gentlemen in evening dress.

"Do you know about their pointed eggs?" asks Pilot Oestensen. "Even a strong wind can't blow them from their place."

"Of course we know," answers Hans-Jakob. "We found one just yesterday, and it's in our bird club collection."

Pilot Oestensen knows more about the auks: As soon as their young ones are old enough to swim the parents push them from the rocks right into the sea.

"It's either sink or swim for them. And the young auks *do* swim, when they are pushed in. Most of them, anyway."

Bird Mountain comes into sight. The sun is not out yet, but the blanket of fog is lifting, and it sails away over the top of the mountain.

We stand at the railing and watch the cliffs: there they are, thousands and thousands of sea gulls sitting all over the face of the mountain and on the ledges as high up as I can see. They fly off and come back, and the air is filled with their screeching. The cliffs and ledges are sprinkled white with their droppings.

"There must be tens of thousands!" I say.

"Call it a million, and you'll come pretty close," Pilot Oestensen tells us. "Our Bird Mountain is the biggest sea gull colony on the whole continent of Europe. Look up there, near the top—two black-coat sea gulls are flying off!" I see them, and then three more.

A swarm of puffins flies past us. They keep very close to the water, and then they dive in and come up again, with another fish added to the collection they already carry in their beaks.

A flight of sea gulls passes over us, shrieking and crying their "kitty-veek" so loudly we can barely hear our own voices.

"Let's try to make them fly off all together!" Paul shouts at the top of his voice.

"Hoo! Hoo! Hoo!" we shout through our cupped hands. "Fly off, you lazybones! Hooooo! Hooooo!"—but the sea gulls pay no attention.

"I will make them fly!" says Pilot Oestensen. He brings a megaphone from his cabin, and blows into it with all he has. "Tooh . . . Tooh . . . Tooh!" it goes, and many sea gulls rise into the air and circle over our heads with angry screeches—but not for long. Soon they settle down again.

Then the engineer comes up on deck, holding a rifle in his hands.

"I'll show you something, boys," he says, and he shoots his rifle into the air. The shot rings out loud, and the powerful echo comes back from Bird Mountain, and now *all* the sea gulls fly up together, and the mountain is bare.

It looks like a million white scraps of paper being thrown up into the sky. Not a single bird is left on Bird Mountain; they are all flying around and around, before they settle down again.

It is a wonderful sight. Now I am sure there were a million, up there in the sunlight.

"How do they find their own nesting places again, I would like to know," Paul says at last.

"One can tell you are not a bird, Flinky!" Hans-Jakob answers. "A bird never goes to the wrong nest!"

The pilot boat glides quickly along the coast, and the lighthouse soon comes within sight. It stands all by itself on the rocks.

We have a rowboat in tow. Pilot Oestensen and we three boys climb down into it and row ashore. The waves toss our boat, and we have to be careful not to capsize. There are dangerous reefs around, but Pilot Oestensen steers us right into an opening between the rocks, and into a quiet little bay.

We run up the cliffs to the lighthouse. There are always two men on duty there. Reidar Goksoeyr is in the engine room, up on the second story. He is working on one of the two Diesel engines that generate the electricity for the light, and Pilot Oestensen gives him the spare parts he needed.

"*God Olav's dag!*" we greet him, and he says:

"Welcome! It's a nice surprise to have young visitors here."

He takes us with him to the top floor. It looks like a giant semi-circular glasshouse, made of hundreds of thick glass panes. They are all prisms. The half-circle is surrounded by a gangway, and then there is another, outer half-circle looking out to the sea. The outer half-circle has open sections and glass sections: some are red, others are green, and between the glass sections, running from top to bottom, are plain black shades. They open and close like regular window shades, and let the light out through the slits, or keep it in when the shades are closed.

The light comes from a single bulb in the center of the inner half-circle. Reidar Goksoeyr switches the bulb on, to show us how the beacon works. It doesn't look very powerful to me.

"The light is magnified thousands of times, as it goes through the prisms of the inner half-circle," Reidar explains. "In passing through the green glass section of the outer half-circle, it floods a large area on the ocean with green light at night. That means OPEN PASSAGE, and ships can be steered safely through this area. But over there are dangerous sandbanks and reefs. This part of the sea is flooded by red lights, and any captain knows that means DANGEROUS WATERS, and keeps away from them."

"Then nothing can ever happen to a ship in this part of the ocean," I say.

"Nothing *should* happen," answers the lighthouse keeper. "But I often remember that horrible night, twelve years ago, when a Finnish cargo ship went aground on the reefs."

"How could that happen, with the red light marking the water?" Paul asks.

"There was no warning light," Reidar Goksoeyr answers. "A terrible storm raged that night in December, the twentieth of December it was, to be exact. The waves were so high that they came up to the very top of the old lighthouse over there, and they smashed the windows. The engines were flooded and stopped working, and so the light went out. It was dreadful. I knew a Finnish cargo boat was due to pass by. I stood there and hoped it would be delayed till morning. But then I saw a tiny blinking light far out on the ocean, and I could do nothing. It came closer and closer. The captain on the ship had no way of knowing he was so near the dangerous coast, because he didn't see any light from my lighthouse.

"I shot red flares into the air, but it was too late. The ship went right into the danger zone, hit a reef, and sank.

"Well, the crew got into the lifeboats and fought their way through the stormy sea toward the shore. They might have struck on the cliffs down here, and have drowned. So I ran down, and shot my red signal flares into the air and warned them off. Then they understood, and went farther east, till they came to the flat beaches at Runde village, and were safe.

"The same year, this new lighthouse was built. It stands much higher than the old one, and farther back from the cliffs. I don't think a storm will ever damage it."

It is getting late, and we have to leave. We say *"God kveld"* to the lighthouse keeper, and walk down to the rowboat, and row out again to the pilot boat.

The sea is calm now, and the sun stands low on the horizon. Thousands and thousands of puffins flit about low over the sea, and dive quickly, and come up again and go on hunting for fish.

We pass the rocks near Bird Mountain. They look dangerous, but Pilot Oestensen knows every one of them, and shows us how close the pilot boat can get to the coast without hitting a rock or a reef.

And then we make straight for home. The sea gulls follow us all the way, till we are back again in the harbor of my village of Runde.

GLOSSARY

Fjells	This is what we call our mountains
Fjords	The long, narrow arms of water reaching inland from the coast of Norway
Frokost	Breakfast
"God dag!"	"Good day!"
"Godt fiske!"	"Good fishing!" We say this as often as "God dag!"
"God kveld!"	"Good night!"
"God morgen!"	"Good morning!"
Hardinglefse	Pancakes—they taste best when they come fresh from the oven, with butter between them
Herre	Mister
Laks	Salmon
Lapskaus	A stew made of meat and potatoes which we eat very often
Middag	Lunch. *Ikke middag* means "no lunch"
Oslo	The capital of Norway. The King has his palace there, and the Parliament meets in Oslo
St. Olav	The patron saint of Norway
Sei	Coalfish
Stikkelsbaer	Gooseberries, which grow behind our house
Torsk	Codfish
"Tusen takk"	"Thousand thanks"

Pronunciation

a	= ah	j	= y
aa	= aw	oe	= or as in *word*
ae	= a as in *hat*	u	= oo

Endpaper maps drawn by Anne Marie Jauss